MW01449867

I HAVE DEVOTED MY LIFE TO THE CLITORIS

# I HAVE DEVOTED MY LIFE TO THE CLITORIS

ELIZABETH HALL

TARPAULIN SKY PRESS
CA ∴ CO ∴ NY ∴ VT
2016

I Have Devoted My Life to the Clitoris
© 2016 Elizabeth Hall
ISBN-13: 978-1-939460-07-3
Printed and bound in the USA

Cover art by Kenyatta A.C. Hinkle. Image courtesy of the Artist and Jenkins Johnson Gallery.

Tarpaulin Sky Press
P.O. Box 189
Grafton, Vermont 05146
www.tarpaulinsky.com

For more information on Tarpaulin Sky Press trade paperback and hand-bound editions, as well as information regarding distribution, personal orders, and catalogue requests, please visit our website at tarpaulinsky.com.

Reproduction of selections from this book, for non-commercial personal or educational purposes, is permitted and encouraged, provided the Author and Publisher are acknowledged in the reproduction. Reproduction for sale, rent, or other use involving financial transaction is prohibited except by permission of the Author and Publisher.

# TABLE OF CONTENTS

| | |
|---|---|
| I HAVE DEVOTED MY LIFE TO THE CLITORIS | 1 |
| THE PATIENT | 11 |
| THE CLITORIS IS SMALL EXCEPT WHEN IT IS NOT | 13 |
| EJACULATION? | 18 |
| CLITS IN THE WILD | 21 |
| RECLAMATION | 23 |
| NAMES | 27 |
| THE ANATOMISTS | 29 |
| THE DOCTORS | 31 |
| MAPPING PLEASURE | 35 |
| THE SEXOLOGISTS | 37 |
| BETTER SEX | 44 |
| OUR BODIES, OURSELVES | 46 |
| FEMALE GENITAL OPERATIONS | 51 |
| DIRTY WORDS | 57 |
| RESEARCH | 60 |
| *SELECTED BIBLIOGRAPHY* | 65 |
| *ACKNOWLEDGEMENTS* | 69 |
| *ABOUT THE AUTHOR* | 71 |

# I HAVE DEVOTED MY LIFE TO THE CLITORIS

- The visible portion of the clitoris is "on average" two to five millimeters in size. Think: stingless honey bee, pomegranate seed, pinkie finger, single English pea.

- The clitoris is small except when it is not.

- Historian Thomas Laqueur writes in his book *Making Sex*, "More words have been shed, I suspect, about the clitoris than about any other organ, or at least about any organ its size."

- *Any organ its size.*

- In her sex memoir, Catherine Millet describes the clitoris as a "sort of muddled knot with no true shape, a minute chaos where two little tongues of flesh meet like when a wave hits the backwash of a second."

- That is, a pleasure so totalizing, wholly satisfying, the body can no longer stand to be a body at all.

- Suppose I were to say I wanted to chart this pleasure, grab hold of its hemline, and follow it slack-jawed, not to better understand it, but to linger, a little longer, within it.

- As early as 1972, psychiatrist Mary Jane Sherfey argued that the clitoris is more than "just the visible tip."

- In 1905 Sigmund Freud published *Three Essays on the Theory of Sexuality* in which he claimed that there were two kinds of female sexualities—the clitoral and the vaginal—with vaginal pleasure being the way adjusted and mature women derive sexual satisfaction. For a woman to achieve maturity, according to Freud, she must transfer her sexual sensation from her clitoris to her vagina.

- "The leading erotogenic zone in female children is located at the clitoris," writes Freud. "All my experience concerning masturbation in little girls has related to the clitoris [...] I am even doubtful whether a female child can be led [...] to anything other than clitoridal masturbation." Clitoral pleasure, for Freud, represented an immature state of sexual development: "Puberty [...] is marked in girls by a fresh wave of repression, in which it is precisely clitoridal sexuality that is affected." However, even in the "adjusted" adult female, Freud felt, the clitoris retained a function, that of transferring sexual pleasure to the vagina, just as "pine shavings can be kindled to set a log of harder wood on fire."

- Freud defined frigidity as the fixation on clitoral (phallic) pleasure instead of the development of vaginal (genital) sexuality.

- In the 1901 version of *Grey's Anatomy* the clitoris was labeled, along with the vulva and vagina. In the 1948 version, the clitoris was actively effaced. Unlabeled, it appears as an unidentifiable black squiggle.

- "There are probably a number of reasons why the clitoris' signifying power has eluded us for so long," writes critic Paula Bennett, "but the most obvious[...]is this issue of size[...]we learn to value that which is large and to dismiss as insignificant as well as inferior when it is small."

- I admit I had expected to unearth a glut of literature, scholarship, and performance art devoted to the clit. My research process was to be a wild romp, every day a delightfully dirty discovery.

- Do not let it disappoint you: I found no museum exhibits Famous Clits in History, nor any Clit Monologues. Instead I discovered, became a collector of, berries, buds, bits of string, petals strewn along the sidewalk.

- *Our Bodies, Ourselves*, published in the eary 1970s, was one of the first post-Freudian women's health guides of its kind. It not only depicted the clitoris in great detail but also a woman looking at her own clitoris. The woman stands over a mirror. Legs spread, slightly bent, she *looks*.

- I thought it was all one color but it's not. Closer and closer the folds appear to be, not a deeper red, but a heavier one, and just inches below the clit, a bright seam of purple flesh throbbing along the lips.

- "The clitoris is coextensive with the detail," writes scholar Naomi Schor. "The clitoral school of feminist criticism might well be identified by its practice of a hermeneutics focused on the detail."

- The rhetorical form of clitoral theory is synecdoche, the "detail-figure," where a single part, or aspect, refers to the whole.

- Ghada Amer's most recognized paintings often consist of a single finely embroidered form repeated over and over linearly on a plain strip of canvas. These "forms" are appropriated from pornographic materials and depict the usual women with their heads tilted back, full beaver spread, rubbing their clitorises or simply just lying there. Sometimes there is cunninlingus, other times firm nipples, a mouth rounded full O. From a distance, however, these pieces resemble the male-dominated abstract expressionism of the past, "improvisational" paint drips and all. But the elaborately detailed forms are often *covered* by said paint drips or, more frequently, a tangle of brightly colored strings. It is only upon closer inspection that one notices the tiny, immaculately embroidered forms at all.

- Embodying both the ornamental and the everyday, the detail is decidedly feminine. Associated with the particular, eccentric, irrational, decadent, prosaic or domestic, the detail stands in firm opposition to classicism, which praised and created a "persistent legacy" for the universal, general or essential. Only after the deconstruction of idealist notions of the cosmic—the "whole"—did the detail gain prominence as an aesthetic category.

- A study in variation, in sameness and difference, artist Hannah Wilke's *176 One-Fold Gestural Sculptures* (1974) was her largest work to date. A 6x8 foot rectangular sea of pink terra cotta forms arranged on a waxed, cherry wood floor: each clay piece, ranging in size from one to five inches, resembled a cunt yet each was unique. Often the only factor distinguishing one cunt from the next was a single fold or gesture.

- Perhaps one balks at the very idea of being but one pussy in a throng of 176 other pussies. I heard on the radio the other day that there are 6.98 billion people in the world. I resigned myself: there are 3.36 billion pussies to keep me company.

- Traditionally, Wilke had displayed the terra cotta cunts, boxes, and blooms she'd been creating since the late 1950's on pedestals. However, at her 1974 one-woman show at Ronald Feldman Gallery, all art work was placed on the floor except one piece, *Needed Erase-Her*, which showcased small folded cunts shaped out of various sized kneaded erasers affixed to 13 ½ inch square boards. Unlike rubber erasers, "kneaded erasers" do not become smaller when used but rather absorb the color of what they have erased, becoming less flexible. Alongside were her "ready-made" fortune cookie pussies.

- According to the artist, she was motivated to create many of the pieces in *Floor Show* by her lover Claes Oldenburg's prolific output as well as his assertion that she "had to do more than one precious piece of sculpture to be an artist."

- For *Laundry Lint* she folded flat lengths of lint collected over the course of two years from Oldenburg's dryer into fifty little cunts arranged in a line against the wall. Red, pink, beige, deep purple, blue: each lint cunt retained remnants of dirt, hair, dust, and clothing labels.

- While it may seem as if we are all universally bound by the same basic needs, desires, lifecycle—we are born, fuck, reproduce, die—this "universality" in and of itself is not the most interesting aspect of this dazzling trip, not even close.

- "It's important for me to make multiple imagery," Wilke said in an interview. "The most subtle differences are very important to me."

- The essential thing about sexual experience is not that we each possess our own specimen, but that nobody knows whether other people also have *this* or something else.

- A connoisseur of small things, sexologist Alfred Kinsey spent sixteen years collecting thousands upon millions of galls while on brutal expeditions to uncut mountains in Mexico and snowy peaks in Colorado. Roughly two milimeters in size, each insect had to be pinned and labeled using a magnifying glass. Beneath the microscope, Kinsey studied every wasp, taking twenty-eight different measurements. What he discovered would change the course of his career: not a single gall was the same.

- Kinsey published his third biology textbook, the massive *The Gall Wasp Genus Cynips: a Study in the Origin of Species* in 1930. At 557 pages the overall theme of the gall specifically, and evolution generally, was individual variation. Although he would not officially begin his studies in human sexuality for eight years, when he did, his approach to his subjects would resemble the method he pioneered with the galls: en masse and in detail. Kinsey noticed even the smallest minutia, such as, during human orgasm "the membranes which line the nostrils may secrete more than their usual amount of mucus."

- Kinsey the rug-maker: imagine him as his daughter Anne describes him, seated on the living room floor, pleating and twisting strips of scrap fabric into thick braid rugs. "He was always making rugs," she says, "[...]listening to the gramophone, sometimes chatting to mother."

- Irises. Kinsey began growing them in 1926. At the peak of his garden, Kinsey grew 150 varieties of 160 known species. Named after the Greek word for rainbow, the flower can be light purple, dark purple, vibrant yellow, faded blue, or a smattering of purple in an otherwise white bloom.

- In his marriage course at the University of Indiana Bloomington, Kinsey took a straightforward tone, often emphasizing basic anatomy and biology. The lectures were well-attended and not without controversy. A colleague, Dr. Thurman Rice, was horrified to learn that Kinsey had been asking female students, in private, about the lengths of their clitorises. Despite pressure from campus prudes, Kinsey continued his research in private.

- According to his biographer Jonathan Gathorne-Hardy, Kinsey rarely slept more than six hours a night and took cold showers in the brittle light of predawn to jolt himself awake. Sleep, what a drag. But to wake before the sun, to see his irises in wild bloom, to return to his research—the wasps, the flushed, convulsing pussies—was the thing itself. Lucky him. For it is a luxury to want to wake up at all.

- Some mornings I can find no good excuse to slip from bed, to feed the cat, to go out and behave in the stinky sunshine except to read on the bus to work a letter Flaubert wrote to Maupassant: "I touch myself when I think of you," signed "Sister Clitoris." This fact, like all my facts, does not tell me anything new about the clitoris or desire, or anything else, but I love it nonetheless.

- Holed-up in a bed with a smashed ankle, scholar Gershon Legman took to paper folding. In 1940 few Westerners knew of the intricate art of origami. A fascinating practice, a kind of alchemy: through a series of tiny and precise creases, a single sheet of paper could morph into an almost infinite number of distinct forms. Legman had been introduced to folding as a child after discovering an illustrated rendition of The Lover's Knot in a magic book. Propped up in bed, he perfected the knot. In the same year, he published his first book *Oragenitalism: Oral Techniques in Genital Excitation for Gentlemen*. What unfolds in this slim, sixty-seven page volume is a beautiful and thoroughgoing testament to clit-licking.

- Better known as a folklorist and dirty joke virtuoso, Legman also peddled Anaïs Nin's dollar a page erotica. In spring of 1940, the pair had a three week affair when Nin was thirty-seven. Nin's biographer, Noel Riley Fitch, claims that, at the age of twenty-three, Legman could be heard saying, "I have devoted my life to the clitoris."

- In a whorehouse outside Louveciennes, Nin herself discovered the clitoris while watching an act of cunnilingus performed by two women: "the little woman loves it [...] The big woman reveals to me a secret place in the woman's body [...] that small core at the opening of the woman's lips, just what the man passed by."

- Legman's first brush with erotica: seated on the floor of his mother's closet, among a forest of perfumed dresses and panties, thumbing through volumes of Havelock Ellis, which she kept with all their "forbidden books" in the back of her wardrobe.

- Perhaps more than any other nineteenth century thinker, Havelock Ellis was the British sexologist, physician, and social reformer responsible for modernizing Western society's sexual beliefs. Although his *Studies in the Psychology of Sex* (1897) contained only passing references (largely anatomical) to the clitoris, Ellis felt that female pleasure was far more diffuse than male pleasure, yet every bit as potent. He was the first sexologist to study homosexuality in depth and without stigmatization. An early advocate of birth control and sexual variation, he himself was turned on by listening to women pee.

- Imagine Nora Joyce sitting in her cramped kitchen reading a routine letter from her husband James: "Tickle your little cockey while you write [...] write the dirty words big [...] and hold them for a moment to your sweet hot cunt...under your dear little farting bum."

- I, too, wish I could lick letters and read them that way. The brain does jizz after all.

- When Gershon Legman published *Oragenitalism* (1940), cunnilingus was still illegal in many US states. One of the most popular marriage manuals at the time—Theodore van de Velde's *Ideal Marriage: Its Physiology and Technique* (1926) — detailed foreplay, including brief mentions of the clitoris, nipples, mouth, and described "the ten sexual positions." According to Van de Velde, oral sex was permitted for foreplay but orgasming from that method was as "pathological" as homosexuality, masturbation, or rear penetration. In this cultural climate, under French pseudonym, Legman wrote his meticulous guide to cunnilingus, devoting passages to nearly every aspect, including the styles of male facial hair best suited for the act: "The beard and the mustache have in common a tendency to sop up the vaginal secretions and, if grey or white, be stained by them. The stain will not show in the dark [or] in blond hair."

- *Oragenitalism* sold few copies so the publisher began offering it as part of a package deal that included a volume of Norman Douglas' erotic limericks and an underground version of Henry Miller's *Tropic of Cancer*. In the year of its publication, almost every copy of *Oragenitalism* was burned when police raided the publisher's headquarters on obscenity charges.

- A ruthless pursuer of minutia, Legman could more accurately be described as having devoted his life to exposing the West's forbidden sexual history. In the 1940's few American scholars' knowledge surpassed his in regard to rare and impossible to find erotic texts as well as dirty jokes, limericks, lewd graffiti, and celebrity and political sex gossip. No matter his subject, his research method remained the same: find everything. Except for a brief stint in the 1960's, he operated outside of academia, leaving the University of Michigan, Ann Arbor in his first semester under the cloud of an unspecified scandal. Instead, he camped out every day for nearly a year at the New York Public Library reading up and through history.

- At train stations across New York, Legman could be found sitting on a bench, folding and refolding a piece of paper, listening to some stranger tell raunchy jokes. Listening was integral to his approach. He often used origami as a way of getting people to open up. Legman was not only interested in the jokes themselves, but also why people told them. He felt that people used jokes as a way of navigating otherwise dangerous or disturbing sexual information. It was during this time that Legman developed his research aesthetic: the careful reintegration of seemingly unrelated details, scraps of forgotten or suppressed knowledge.

- In 1943 Kinsey hired Legman as the Institute of Sex Research's first official bibliographer. The pair met through Legman's former employer, Robert Latou Dickinson, a pioneering gynecologist and birth control advocate who contributed greatly to the modernization of sex. Although Dickinson was eighty-two at the time, he was extremely proud of the fact he could still orgasm two or three times a year with the help of a patient female assistant.

- Dickinson was a priceless resource for Kinsey. In 1949 Dickinson wrote him a letter about a town in deep Kansas where the women were reputed to have orgasms very easily and almost always. When Kinsey visited the town, he discovered that the parents soothed their female babies by massaging the genital area, which often led to a quieting orgasm. Kinsey felt their orgasmic habits were a learnt reaction carried through to adulthood.

- If the idea of comforting your baby, or any baby, via this method turns your stomach, don't fret. Your baby, and many other babies, will soon learn to soothe themselves, in more or less the same manner, all on their own. If lucky, they will never forget.

# THE PATIENT

- When Sigmund Freud met Marie Bonaparte, he was sixty-nine, and he referred to her first and always as Princess. Within a matter of weeks, they met every day. Eleven a.m. to one p.m. All formalities dissolved. Marie confided in Freud, Freud confided in Marie. After three weeks, he confessed: "Look…I'm telling you more than to other people after two years…I must also add that I am not a connoisseur of human beings."

- A year earlier Marie had conducted her own clitoral research, developing an idiosyncratic theory of female frigidity that emphasized a biological root. After measuring the distance between the clitoris and the vagina in 243 women during routine gynecology examinations, Marie concluded that women with short distances (the "paraclitoridiennes") achieved orgasm easily during intercourse while women with a distance of more than two and a half centimeters (the "téléclitoridiennes") did not.

- Marie considered herself téléclitoridienne. In her essay "Considerations on the Anatomical Causes of Frigidity in Women" (1924), she wrote: "Even if [an] attentive lover is found and his caresses […] lead to orgasm, these women will never be fully satisfied."

- And where might this one, true satisfaction lie? Marie focused on the connection between the clitoris and the vagina, their proximity, intricate kinesis. Although she pursued many men, her lovers failed to satisfy her sexually. Frigid? No, Marie knew how to come. But orgasm, and orgasm alone, was not it. Marie wanted to come during penetration, from penetration. With her lover inside her.

- In 1926 Marie underwent a procedure performed by Dr. Josef von Halban to move her clitoris closer to her vagina. The operation took twenty-two minutes. Although it proved ineffective, she continued to champion the procedure among colleagues and friends as well as in published reports. The following year, with only local anesthesia, Marie endured another operation. And another. But the sensitivity in the place from where the clitoris had been moved persisted.

- I prefer to imagine that Marie opted for no more than local anesthesia so that she could watch the doctor as he tinkered. That she, too, liked to look.

- Freud disapproved of Marie's operations, calling them "your heroic surgeries" in his letters, and instructed her to "turn her focus inward."

- On this point, however, they agreed: often it is less about what one hopes to find so much as the thrill of the hunt itself.

- Marie's lifelong search for a vaginal orgasm was, in a way, not at all related to the orgasm itself, but rather, the desire to feel it, in the same instant, with another. That's the terror: when you don't.

## THE CLITORIS IS SMALL EXCEPT WHEN IT IS NOT

- Often I have longed for a single exquisite fuck cataclysmic enough to permanently snuff all the *other* needs of my body: eating, sleeping, not sleeping, shitting, or, for one, the need to be touched all over, all at once, when there is no one but me in the apartment.

- The clitoris possesses 8,000 nerve endings and consists of three major parts: the glans, body, and crura. The erectile portions are composed of the cavernous and vestibule bulbs.

- When in the midst of an otherworldly migraine, or eight-day insomnia haze, I endure a near constant communion with my body: I am aware of its immense powers, limitations, ability to humiliate my intelligence entirely. No sooner do I feel as if I have "figured it out," could predict the onset of a migraine down to the most infinitesimal detail, do I find myself leveled out in bed, face spangled with sweat, hair slicked with vomit. I must submit, let myself go with it, knowing I will emerge, as with many of life's most lonely and degrading things, having learned nothing whatsoever.

- If there is any sort of epiphany, "convalescent euphoria," that accompanies such pain, it does not stem from the ache itself, but rather, my release from it. What no drug, practiced "mind over matter" technique can accomplish: I let my finger linger over and around my clit, and with the first flush, feel the happy little ants dancing in the tip top notch of my cunt, down my legs, onto my feet. No matter that the pain will return in mere minutes. To have felt such freedom, any release at all.

+ The clitoral shaft, which feels like a piece of cord, is attached to the glans and rises underneath the skin towards the mons. When aroused, I roll my finger across it for extra pleasure. At the top of the shaft, it splits; two legs curve downward, like a wishbone. These are called *crura*, or legs. It is not possible to see or feel the legs. Although I have tried.

+ After years of consciousness-raising workshops and research, the Federation of Feminist Women's Health Clinics (FFWHC) published *A New View of a Woman's Body: An Illustrated Guide* (1991) in which the term "clitoris" encompasses *all* eighteen structures that undergo changes during the orgasmic cycle.

+ Studying two fresh and eight fixed human female adult cadavers, using MRI technology, Australian doctor Helen O'Connell discovered that the clitoris extends far into the body, its spindly nerve endings spooling out, a swath of erectile tissue lining the vagina walls, vestibule.

+ In 1998 O'Connell published her results in *The Journal of Urology*: "The vaginal wall is, in fact, the clitoris. If you lift the skin off the vagina on the side walls, you get the bulbs of theclitoris-triangular, crescental masses of erectile tissue [...] *current anatomical description of female human urethral and genital anatomy is inaccurate.*"

+ O'Connell's research was a breakthrough not because it asserted the existence of the "complete clitoris"; feminists had been arguing that for decades. Rather, it was viewed by a skeptical medical community as proving, for the first, the existence of the complete clitoris via the hard science of MRI technology.

- The size of the clitoral hood varies from complete coverage to wide-open visibility. When the clitoris is turned on, it swells, often emerging from the hood. Shortly before you climax, it retracts. At the onset of puberty, the clitoral glans becomes on average one-and-a-half times larger, and after menopause, it can grow as much as two and a half times larger than at age nineteen. During menopause the clitoris may also retreat, disappearing entirely beneath the hood. None of this effects how it *feels*, only how it looks.

- In his novel *Tropic of Cancer*, Henry Miller claimed he could see the whole of the world in the fucked out cunt of a whore.

- When I gaze deep inside a pussy, that's all I see: a pussy. That is enough.

- As Gertrude Stein might have said, a clit is a clit is a clit.

- Except when it is not. Consider the female spotted hyena, an animal known for its "enlarged clitoris," extending, during childbirth, up to seven inches from her body. Spotted hyenas live in clans and are a matriarchy. They have sex, urinate, and give birth through their clitoris. In order to attract a female hyena in heat, males adopt submissive behavior. Hyena sex isn't easy: it takes careful positioning for the male to crouch behind and point his penis up and backwards to enter the female's clitoris. Much of the medical literature refers to the hyena's clitoris as a "pseudo-penis" with dominant behavior often described as "male-like." Such aggressive behavior is thought to result from an influx of androgen, an "androgen bath," during the last phases of gestation.

- The hyena's transgressive nature was known to pre-Islamic Arabic poets. In such texts, hyenas are routinely depicted as breaching a vast array of social mores: killing and feasting upon gracious hosts, menstruating out in the open, laughing all the while; when a pack of hyenas wander upon a dead warrior, they pleasure themselves with his still stiff cock.

- In *The Physiologus*—written in Egypt around 200-400 C.E., translated into Greek and Latin and widely available throughout the West—the hyena is portrayed as an "alternating male-female[...]unclean because it has two natures."

- In the early 2000s, a research team, Berkley Hyena Project (BHP), led by Dr. Laurence G. Frank, received ample funding to trace the role of androgens in the development of the spotted hyena's "female phallus." Early in their studies, BHP concluded: "it has become clear that the spotted hyena's genitals are a result of a prenatal exposure to androgens." Instead of viewing this "androgen bath" as an evolutionarily beneficial aspect of the hyenas, BHP tends to interpret it as an evolutionary oops. A team of German researchers, meanwhile, argue that the erectile clitoris was selected and functions to restrain male control of reproduction: forced copulations for the female spotted hyena are impossible because they have sex via *penetration of the clitoris*, which requires a great deal of patience and precision. Females thus gain control over the mechanism of copulation and male mating success becomes dependant on the relationships they develop with females.

- Researcher Anna Wilson writes, "The hyena has moved from being the dangerous, unknowable other into a position of that which can be known, studied, and dissected but that is still other."

- Human anatomy is often thought to be a dead field of inquiry, one in which the essential truths about the body were established long ago. But what of the art of anatomy? A creative practice subject to the same joys, prejudices, and false revelations as any artistic undertaking.

- For years I lived under the delusion that the way I viewed my body was identical to the way that doctors, cultural theorists, lovers, et cetera viewed it. That is, I struggled to understand that the body I had inhabited for years—that I had come to see as *mine*—was not at all the same body that others saw. Many did not even see it as "mine." Once aware of this disconnect, however, my delusion did not end: I thought it did not matter.

# EJACULATION?

- Before the explosion of internet porn, The British Board of Film Classification (BBFC) was responsible for regulating films seeking classification as R18, which meant they could be sold to licensed sex shops. On May 2001, the BBFC passed *Squirt Queens* (retitled *British Cum Queens*) only after excising six minutes and twelve seconds of an actress ejaculating during orgasm. According to the committee, the scene constituted urolagnia, banned since 1959 by the Obscene Publications Act. The BBFC board stated, "expert medical advice informed us that there is no such thing as 'female ejaculation' and that the fluid present in *Squirt Queens* was in fact urine." They did not believe that the film showed female ejaculation because, to them, the very act itself was impossible. Their loss.

- The first pussy I saw up close belonged to an aging barfly named Alana, and it looked nothing like my own. While my cunt was the definition of a slit—long slim lips shoring up a compact clit, puritan in its lack of ornamentation—Alana's pussy was a florid, almost hairless, forest of folds. I wasn't sure what to do when I pushed her panties to the side, how long to continue. I simply licked each fold till they began to wriggle, fan out, then circled back to her clit. She tilted her head, "Ah." And just like that— a clear, briny dew filled my mouth. It was not, as some say, the nectar of gods; more, the gleam at the end of the forest.

- Although I had spent the first twenty or so years of my life unaware that women could ejaculate—or, at least, produce the strong, visible streams so associated with male orgasm—I did not need anyone to explain what had happened with Alana. I did not need to read a book: I was there.

- One of the first thorough studies on the female prostate was published in 1948 by gynecologist John W. Huffman who discovered that the tissue surrounding the urethra contained prostatic-like glands (found in male uretha) near the urethral opening; one model had up to thirty-one glands.

- Named after Dr. Ernst Grafenberg, a German gynecologist, the G-spot was originally thought to be solely responsible for female ejaculation. This view was advanced in the 1982 book *The G-Spot*, which introduced the highly sensitive area to the mainstream; however, as later discovered, ejaculation can accompany any kind of orgasm. Grafenberge wrote, "large quantities of a clear, transparent fluid are expelled not from the vulva, but out of the urethra in gushes."

- In her book *Eve's Secrets: A New Theory of Female Sexuality* (1987), Josephine Sevely documented the extensive history of female ejaculation, arguing that the phenomenon was well-known to societies across the world from antiquity to the 19th century.

- Vladimir Nabokov knew: in his novel *Ada or Ardor*, set in the late 19th century, two teen girls (also sisters) play a game called "pressing the spring" by "interweaving like serpents" and "kissing her *krestik*."

- The *corpus spongiosum*, G-spot, and urethral sponge all refer to the same swath of tissue, which are included in the Federation of Feminist Women's Health Clinic's definition of the "complete clitoris."

- Alice Kahn Ladas, Beverly Whipple and John Perry (1980's) found that many women produce a clear, alkaline fluid that is not urine which may vary in amount from a few drops to two ounces, sometimes up to eight ounces. They also found that prostatic acid phosphatase (PAP), an enzyme found in male prostatic secretions, and glucose were "substantially higher in the ejaculatory fluid [of women] than in urine samples."

- In 1997 Spanish researchers Francisco Cabello Santamaria and Rico Nesters analyzed the urine of twenty-four women before and after orgasm for the presence of prostate-specific antigen (PSA). Unlike the preograsmic urine samples, seventy-five percent of the postograsmic samples showed a concentration of PSA. In the fluid emitted at the height of orgasm, one hundred percent of the samples contained PSA. All women are capable of ejaculation, but the amount may be too little to notice. Even if they look very close.

- Performer Carol Queen wrote in *Exhibitionism for the Shy* that her ejaculate tasted like buttered popcorn, sometimes the forest floor, while Fanny Fatale reported that hers had no smell.

- A lover once wrote in a poem that I tasted like scorched marmalade, but he was a romantic.

## CLITS IN THE WILD

- The closest I come to romance, to anything resembling coquetry, is to walk down the street in the summer heat, sans panties, letting the heavenly stench of my pussy fan out into the atmosphere. It's how I prefer to wander: cunt pressed to the skin of the city.

- Other animals do it differently. The "winking effect" refers to a mating ritual performed by female heifers and mares in heat. When a male stern or stallion comes close, the female's clitoris retracts under the hood then swells out again. As he takes another step closer, the clitoris retracts yet again, then the labia relaxes, and the clitoris slips out. The ultimate come-hither.

- Certain mammals such as the cat and rabbit require mechanical stimulation of the clitoris, vulva, and vagina in order to ovulate. In the practice of artificial insemination of cattle, it is well-known that stimulating the clitoris will induce immediate response.

- In his novel *Lady Chatterley's Lover*, D.H. Lawrence describes the clitoris as a bird's beak waiting to attack: "By God, you think a woman's soft down there, like a fig. But I tell you [they] have beaks between their legs, and they tear at you with it till you're sick."

- Stump-tailed Macaque moms often comfort their infants, male or female, by rhythmically stroking the infant's genitalia.

- Look around: female dogs that are not in heat will rub their clitorises on any suitable object until some seemingly pleasurable resolution is reached.

- It does not depend on season. Days when even the scent of the rain-slicked sidewalk makes my pussy dewy. Stuck in traffic on the freeway, I can't be bothered to wait. Sun wet on my thighs: I slide my hand up my skirt, press my legs together, and rub and rub my little roundlet till it succumbs. Because I can.

- Masturbation is also frequent in female dolphins of any age, and clitoral stimulation is sought during play with other dolphins of both sexes.

- If the clitoris, as is often articulated in modern thought, serves no reproductive functions, perhaps it might be more useful to think of the ways in which its assumed function—pleasure—might be adaptive. How the capacity to experience and self-generate limitless physical pleasure might in itself prove to be an evolutionary benefit.

# RECLAMATION

- In the *American Journal of Obstetrics and Gynecology*, two Italian obstetricians published their observations, via ultra-sound examination, of "a female fetus at 32 weeks gestation touching [her] vulva with the fingers of [her] right hand. The caressing movement was centered primarily on the clitoris. Movements stopped after 30 to 40 seconds, and started again after a few moments. Further, these light touches were repeated and were associated with short, rigid movements of the pelvis and legs. After another break, in addition to this behavior, the fetus contracted the muscles of the trunk and limbs, and the climax, [rapid muscle contractions], of the body followed."

- Non-reproductive sexual behavior has been observed in almost every mammal. According to researcher Ina Jane Wundram, the protozoa were early inventors of sexual reproduction, "having learned to come together in pairs to swap genetic information before separating to divide into daughter cells." However, protozoa can also reproduce asexually through simple cell division; sexual behavior is not a prerequisite for reproduction. "Whether there is any "non-reproductive sex" in protozoa is uncertain because of our poor understanding of the meaning of "sexual" here," writes Wundram. But there is a process called "autogamy" where the protozoan builds a protective cyst or wall around itself and "undergoes changes as if it is preparing for sexual union with another protozoan." That is—it splits its nuclear material into macronuclei and micronuclei but instead of exchanging micronuclei with another of its kind, it "autogamizes"—allows the two subnuclei to reunite. "The cyst opens," writes Wundram, "and this same protozoan swims forth invigorated, as if somehow revitalized by the process."

- The Greek *Kleitoriazein*, means to "touch" or "titillate" lasciviously, to be inclined to pleasure.

- I was not a natural masturbator in that the act of getting off did not occur to me instinctually. I had to *read* about it in a book. It was not that I thought masturbation was wrong or that I thought people did not do it or that I didn't understand the basic mechanics—I had not gotten that far. It had simply never occurred to me that the action might appeal to me, specifically. That my body was capable of such pleasure at all.

- Dorothy Allison's *Bastard Out of Carolina* tells the story of pain, generations of pain, as manifested in the personal story of Bone, a young girl growing up in 1950's Greenville, South Carolina. When her mother remarries, her stepfather, the monstrous Daddy Glen, begins sexually and physically abusing her, at one point even breaking her tailbone. Yet amidst all the horror—brief moments of bliss when Bone slips her hand between her legs and comes so hard the whole world burns up, if only for an instant.

- In the woods, behind their rented clapboard, Bone climbs to the very top of a tree while her younger sister Reese, unaware of her presence, plays out her personal pleasure ritual: a white sheet tied round her neck like a cape, she rolls around on the ground, in the wet leaves, dirt, stray twigs, saying *no! no!* her face streaked with terror. From her perch, Bone watches: "I hugged myself tightly to the tree and rocked my hips against the indifferent trunk. I imagined I was tied to the branches above and below me. Someone had beaten me with dry sticks and put their hands in my clothes [...] Below me Reese, pushed her hips into the leaves and made grunting sounds. Someone, someone, she imagined, was doing terrible, exciting things to her."

- In mainstream media—books, magazines, tv, movies, et cetera—the pleasure of sex is almost always depicted within the context of romantic love or uncontrollable lust and not, say, the sensation of orgasm itself. That is, the pleasure of orgasm, in my head, became something almost exclusively dependent upon another person. It was not until I was twenty, living in a cramped attic apartment alone, still a "choosy" virgin, watching, for the first, hours upon hours of internet porn, that I realized the sensation itself might be *it*.

- In her diaries, personal letters, and conversations with close friends, Simone de Beauvoir often referred to memoirist Violette Leduc as "the ugly one." Although de Beauvoir admired Leduc's writing, and launched her career, she found her to be impossibly annoying and cloying. Leduc was aware (oh, how precisely aware) of her shortcomings. In fact, she fashioned a sort of triumph out of her ugliness: "I wanted to be a hard focus of attention for the customers in a cafe, for the audience in a music-hall lounge, because I was ashamed of my face and because I wanted to force it upon them at the same time."

- Similar to Dorothy Allison's texts, Leduc's memoirs contain much personal terror, interrupted by the joy of a buttered biscuit or sliver of beef; a slash of light in a room dark otherwise at noon; the clitoris: "A light is in my limbs[...]I burgle my sex. I plunder my caresses. I steal what belongs to me."

- According to Edna St. Vincent Millay's sister, Norma, Edna rushed into her room late one night in the apartment they shared in Greenwich Village, and said that there was "a little piece of flesh between my legs and I should rub it back and forth. And when I thought I couldn't stand it anymore, then I should keep rubbing it."

- It is not that every time I come, I tread the infinite. It is enough to feel as if I am the highest hollyhock on the stem.

- My body is all I've ever had.

# NAMES

- The *OED* puts a double-bar in front of the entry for clitoris, meaning "not naturalized in English," i.e. the word clitoris is not considered common parlance. Outside of the abbreviated "clit," originating in the 1950's, there are no wide-spread common slang-terms, no clit colloquialisms.

- As a girl, imagine having read—not just in a smutty mag pilfered from someone else's stash—but in a teen rag, or better yet, note passed between girlfriends in class, a single reference to the clit as "stiff," as having a "hard on"—that is, a thing to be touched, plumbed and plundered, "jerked off."

- More specific, descriptive, and delicious than a full page color photograph: rub one off.

- There is no word for clitoris in ancient Greek, and the first time the word *kleitoris* appears, it is as an anatomical term in Rufus of Ephesus texts. Rufus of Ephesus, writing around the first and second century AD, lists the word *kleitoris* alongside three other synonyms, only two of which were still used during his time: *numoe*, a metaphor whose sense is "the veiled" and *murton*, "myrtle berry," based on the appearance of that berry.

- Found in a fragment attributed to Plutarch, the word *klitoris* also describes a dark-colored stone worn as an earring by the natives who live along the Indus River.

- The German *der kitxler*, interchangable with *der klitoris*, translates roughly as "the tickler."

- Fifteen terms existed in Latin for clitoris, and the ancient Romans had medical knowledge of the clitoris; their native word for it was *landica*. There is some evidence that it may have been one of the most obscene words in the Latin lexicon. It is alluded to, but does not appear, in literary sources, except in the *Priapeia* 79, which calls it *misella landica*, the "poor little clitoris." It does, however, appear in graffiti.

- Allusions to the clitoris in the Satires of Juvenal call it *crista*, "crest."

- The word cunnilingus also occurs in literary Latin and is found once in Catullus, and more frequently in Martial; it denotes the person who performs the action, not the action itself, as in modern English, where it is not obscene but technical. The term comes from the Latin word for the vulva (*cunnus*) and the verb "to lick" (*linguere*, *lingua* "tongue")

# THE ANATOMISTS

- During the centuries preceding the sixteenth century, the clitoris was not lost so much as lost in translation. Due to the linguistic imprecision of their Arabic sources, and the slippery terminology of the Latin translators, medical texts of the time tended to identify the clitoris with the labia minor, or to view it as a pathological growth.

- 1559: Renaldo Columbus, a lecturer in surgery at the University of Padua, rediscovered the clitoris while studying female patients and elderly cadavers. Rediscovered: he *described* the clitoris.

- "So pretty and useful a thing," Columbus wrote in his book *De Re Anatomica*. "Since no one has discerned these projections and their workings, if it is permissible to give names to things discovered by me, it should be called the love or sweetness of Venus [...] if you touch it you will find it rendered a little harder and oblong to such a degree it shows itself as a sort of male member."

- Not long after the publication of *De Re Anatomica*, Fallopius, a student of Columbus, argued in his book that he, and he alone, had discovered the clitoris: "any others who speak or write about this [the clitoris] be assured that they learned of the thing itself either from me or my followers."

- A century later, noted anatomist Kasper Bartholin scoffed at both Fallopius and Columbus: the clitoris had been *known to everyone* since the second century.

- And before the second century? If a woman orgasms clitorally in a forest and no one is around to hear it, does it happen?

- Columbus' account, however, is significant: it assumes that looking and touching will reveal different truths about bodies.

- As Jane Sharp's 1610 midwives manual confirms: the clitoris, like the glans of the penis, "will stand and fall [...] makes woman lustful [...] were it not for this they would have no desire nor delight, nor would they conceive."

- It is largely impossible to know what those outside the medical community thought about the clitoris in early and modern Western history as many texts "of the people" such as midwives handbooks and marriage manuals did not survive. Impossible, that is, to say how many women sprawled atop straw mattresses and kneaded their little nubbins until dizzy, constellations of sweat beneath their breasts.

# THE DOCTORS

- According to Thomas Lacquer, most Western anatomists abided by the One Sex Model for thousands of centuries, and that One Sex was male. In this view, first formulated by Galen, female genitalia was seen as analogous to male genitalia; the female was simply turned inward with the clitoris representing the glans of the penis.

- In his two part treatise *Gynaecology* (first/second century), Soranus, a physician from Ephesus, addressed a variety of topics including, but not limited to, the anatomy of the female reproductive organs, qualities of a good midwife, descriptions of the child birthing process, a guide to newborn care, and information on uterine growths. The chapter entitled *"Concerning Immensely Great Clitoris and Clitoridectomy [sic]"* advocated the surgical removal of a part of the woman's clitoris if it was "overly large," a behavior Soranus associated with unrestrained sexual behavior.

- The word *Clitorizonte*, a variant of the Greek *Kleitorebeis*, meant to "rub lasciviously." Some also defined it as "trying lascivious sport with other women."

- The term *tribad* embodied many meanings ranging from women with large clitorises to those who actively sought sex with other women to those who were mentally ill. The most popular treatments for tribadism during this time were mind control and selective clitoridectomy. In his *On Acute and Chronic Diseases*, Sonorus recommended clitoridectomies for women who behaved like men. He also posited the influential argument that tribads were incurable because their problem was rooted in the soul, not the body.

- During the Middle Ages through the modern period, surgeons in Europe were educated in the art of performing "selective clitoridectomy" on women with an "overly large clitoris."

- The typical "selective clitoridectomy" procedure in the nineteenth century: the woman lies on her back, legs together. The surgeon holds the excess part of the clitoris with a small forcep then cuts back the clitoris with a scalpel. The legs must be kept together to avoid cutting too much.

- Aetius of Amida, a Christian physician writing in Greek in the early sixth century, discussed clitordectomies using Philoumenos, a second century medical writer, as his source. He described three main reasons for the procedure: an overly large clitoris, to relieve clitoral adhesions, and to release fluid built up within a diseased or cancerous clitoris. Aetius asserted that an enlarged clitoris will inevitably lead to licentious behavior due to the constant rubbing of the clitoris against undergarments which "stimulates the desire for intercourse."

- Sinistrari, a Roman inquisitor of the early sixteenth century, claimed that women with elongated clitorises could rape men or engage in "sodomy" with other women.

- In sixteenth century France, "hermaphrodite" could mean as little or as much as "large clitoris," up to the size of a "small finger." Prompted by two recent court cases, anatomist Jean Riolan published an essay arguing that so-called hermaphrodites were *really nothing more* than women with enlarged clitorises.

- According to the French surgeon and anatomist Duvel (1600's), it was not exclusively the clergy and law officials who prompted clitoral surgeries but the girls themselves for "fear of becoming a popular tale."

- One such tale: Marie Lange, described as a hermaphrodite with a seven inch clitoris, who was on exhibition throughout Paris and London in 1777.

- A voice of reason: Parent-Duchatelet's 1857 study of Parisian prostitutes disclosed that the clitoris "was found to be of normal size in females of the most unbridled passions."

- Not until the mid-nineteenth century did the causal connection between hysteria ("nervous diseases") and clitoral masturbation become widespread. Nineteenth century surgeons were not concerned with the size of the clitoris so much as its capacities for personal pleasure.

- *The Lancet*, a British medical journal, reported that in Berlin in 1822 Dr. Graefe performed a clitoridectomy on a supposedly "idiotic" fourteen-year-old patient with a medical history of excessive masturbation and nymphomania. The surgery was reported as a success in that all "self pollution" stopped although "a few suspicious motions, the remains of a long-continued habit, were occasionally observed."

- I imagine—and imagine is all I can do—that these doctors, too, had experience with "the long continued habit." Knew intimately of its dangers, the almost intolerable splendor of letting the body alone to seek and find what it likes.

- Excision as a cure for masturbation was noted in Paris as early as 1812. Prior to the mid-nineteenth century, female masturbation was rarely discussed, and when it was, the cures for "self pollution" included such benign measures as vigorous exercise, hot baths, hard mattresses, and a more prudent diet.

- Declitorization reached a peak in the West in 1860's with Isaac Baker Brown, a London-based obstetrician, who performed and avidly recommended clitoridectomies as a cure for masturbation, epilepsy, and various symptoms of hysteria. At the time many prominent surgeons subscribed to the Psychology of the Ovary theory, linking all medical and emotional problems in women to their malfunctioning ovaries. Brown's success with the ovariotomy procedure he pioneered, including one he had performed on his sister, established his reputation.

- Brown founded his own hospital in 1858, and seven years later, was elected President of the Medical Society of London. Brown felt that all the conditions listed in the title of his book *On the Curability of Certain Forms of Insanity, Epilepsy, Catalepsy, and Hysteria in Females* (1866) could potentially be cured by excising the clitoris. Although the book was later condemned, and Brown disgraced, few critics opposed the biological determinism behind his procedure.

## MAPPING PLEASURE

- In the late eighteenth century, anatomists began illustrating some of the first explicitly female skeletons in order to show how the differences between men and women could be explained via anatomy.

- Imagine the thrill: to know all there was to know about your lover—their needs, fears, humiliations laid bare in startling clarity—simply by measuring, charting, looking and looking again at their naked body in a shaft of sun.

- "It was not until 1759 that anyone bothered to reproduce a detailed female skeleton in an anatomy book to illustrate its difference from the male," writes Lacquer. "And when the differences were discovered they were already, in the very form of their representation, deeply marked by the power politics of gender."

- In 1844 Georg Ludwig Kobelt published his sprawling anatomy text *The Male and Female Organs of Sexual Arousal* that described the clitoris' structure and function in exquisite detail.

- Exquisite detail: the clitoris is a difficult organ to study post-mortem, but Kobelt had devised a technique for injecting the vasculature of the clitoris so that it could be studied with precision. "[Due to] the small number of nerves [in] the voluminous vagina," Kobelt wrote, "we can grant the vagina no part in the creation of […] the pleasurable sex feelings in the female body."

- British psychiatrist Henry Savage published *The Surgery, Surgical Pathology and Surgical Anatomy of the Female Pelvic Organs* (1870), one of the first modern anatomy texts to describe the clitoris using active language such as "extends" "come together" and "sudden turn forward."

- More representative of his contemporaries than Kobelt or Savage, sexologist Richard von Krafft-Ebing asserted that the "normal" and "civilized" female possessed a "small sexual desire." He regarded female passivity in the public sphere as inherently imbedded in their "sexual organization." While describing the many erogenous zones in the female, including the nipples, he wrote, "the erogenous zones in the women are, while she is a virgin, the clitoris, and after defloration, the vagina and cervix uteri."

- It seems Kraft-Ebbing also dreamed of a single, exquisite fuck potent enough not only to rearrange the furniture of a woman's brain or, say, the way the sun slants on her window sill, but a fuck so intoxicating as to irrevocably alter the actual way her body functions, interprets pleasure—that is, nothing short of a total revolution.

- And for some it is. They fuck and feel as if they've touched upon some elemental truth about humanity. I confess: the first time I fucked paled in comparison to the first *touch* wherein I spent hours pressed flush against a stranger's immaculate nakedness as the afternoon sweat itself out. I could remain unfucked forever, but *this* I knew I would devote my life to.

# THE SEXOLOGISTS

- Although Havelock Ellis was perhaps the first widely read "modernizer of sex," Robert Latou Dickinson also played a major role in liberalizing Western sexual attitudes. In 1931 Kinsey read Dickinson's *A Thousand Marriages: A Medical Study of Sex Adjustment*. Ten years later, he wrote to Dickinson that it was *A Thousand Marriages* that first gave him the idea that he might "research in this field [sexuality]."

- Dickinson believed that an effective medical practice hinged on detailed patient histories. During his most active years as an obstetrician and gynecologist (1890-1920), patients were required to fill out a four-page questionnaire. As he examined each woman, he made at least five drawings of the uterus, cervix, and vulva. The maximum number of drawings for any one patient was sixty one. As photography became widespread, he supplemented the drawings with photographs. His standard practice was to read the patient's answers to the questionnaire and use them to question her further. These interviews served as the source material for *A Thousand Marriages*, in which he described the analysis of one thousand cases.

- Dickinson also published the groundbreaking *Atlas of Human Sexuality* (1949) in which he introduced normalizing models of the human body named Norma and Normann.

Along with meticulous descriptions of the clitoris and hundreds of images, he stressed sexual agency: "Orgasm is orgasm however achieved."

- Despite the dedicated work of these sex radicals, and outsiders such as Magnus Hirschfeld, most of the medical community followed Freud's model of female frigidity. With the publication of Kinsey's *Sexual Behavior in the Human Male* (1948) that model was forever shattered.

- *Sexual Behavior in the Human Male* was a sensation, both attacked and lauded by all of the major news publications. Even actress Mae West longed to meet the famous scientist, sending a telegram to his hotel: "Anxious to meet you please telephone me."

- In terms of pure style, Kinsey felt that *Sexual Behavior in the Human Female* (1953) was superior to the male. With the latter, he had written and painstakingly edited it largely himself, often fretting over punctuation; in the proofs, "perhaps" is changed to "certainly" then "inevitably." For *Sexual Behavior in the Human Female*, Kinsey enlisted, and actually accepted, advice. There were also multiple authors. When editor Emily Mudd suggested he rethink his use of "failure" in sentences such as females' "failure to be aroused," he changed it to "lack." However, despite many staff objections, Kinsey continued to refer to the female human, as he had done with the male, with the biologically correct term "animal."

- What does it mean to "fuck like an animal?" Perhaps one imagines two dogs on the side of the road, bare asses bobbing in the weeds, no thoughts, just the wildness of their bodies; or a heifer in early spring, winking her clit at any passing fancy, driven to fuck solely by the right scent, season, never this headache of trying to do right by feelings.

- But what is lost when we take sanctuary in such stories?

What of the randy macaque who is willing to trade his most precious possession—food or juice—for a single glimpse of a female monkey's bare bottom? As Chinese zookeepers recently discovered, Giant Pandas will not mate in captivity; they're persnickety. However, since giant pandas are an endangered species, zookeepers needed them to reproduce so they began showing them blue movies of pandas, doing it, in the jungle. The films worked: the pandas did not fuck "as in the wild," but they fucked.

+ The point, here, is not "they're just like us!" or that, once we understand the nuances of animal sexuality, we will learn something important about human desire, but rather, that we can know *why* they do what they do, but not if they feel any blister of pleasure, or what that pleasure might mean to them.

+ Kinsey's *Sexual Behavior in the Human Female* sold out in six weeks. Its coverage in the press surpassed that of *Sexual Behavior in the Human Male*, but the team's findings were every bit as startling. Although it was known that women could experience multiple orgasms, it was not widely documented or described until Kinsey's study. It was also fairly common. Thirteen percent of Kinsey's sample could have multiple orgasms. The number and intensity varied.

+ One volunteer, Alice Dent, could come within two to five seconds and experience orgasm fifteen to twenty times in twenty minutes. A pornographer's dream?

+ In his masturbation sample of adult women, Kinsey found that 85% lightly stroked or stimulated (in various ways) the labia minora and clitoris. Only 20% used vaginal penetration and always in conjunction with some other method. The team also found that women masturbating or making love with other women, came quickly, or quicker than men; 45% in three minutes or less, 25% in four to five minutes.

- Although Kinsey reported that the vaginal orgasm was a "biological impossibility," he felt that the whole sex (vagina, nipples, clit, mouth, etc) was important. Highlighting the perineal nervous system, he wrote, "contractions of the anal sphincter appear to produce contractions of muscles in various remote parts of the body, including areas as far away as the throat and nose."

- That is the wager, isn't it? To fuck your lover—or anyone—so that they experience pleasure in the most obscure wings of their body?

- Kinsey's study was largely a success but some found it despicable. Although he did not actually read the female volume, Baptist pastor Billy Graham declared, "It is impossible to estimate the damage this book will do to the already deteriorating morals of America." Anthropologist Margaret Mead felt that the book's publication "left many young people singularly defenseless in just those areas where their desire to conform was protected by a lack of knowledge."

- As if critical inquiry into sex would forever strip fucking of its magic, romance, power. But there are other romances, too. For me, the tease, the romance of seeking.

- Crouched, with one eye lifted, Bill Masters squinted into a small, lit hole bored into a hotel wall. However, this was no ordinary peep show. Masters, a celebrated fertility specialist, was researching the human sexual response, a project he had begun in 1955 by interviewing and observing prostitutes with their clients in dim-lit dives throughout St. Louis. In 1956 he moved his studies into the controlled settings of a laboratory at Washington University. However, a single question changed the course of his research forever: "What if I fake it?" asked a female participant, a biology graduate and part-time sex worker. Masters blinked at her, said flatly, "I don't know what you mean." She replied, "That's what I do for a living." He remained dumbfounded, "I simply could not understand her [...] I'm not sure I ever did."

- Within weeks Masters hired Virginia Johnson, a twice-divorced mother of two, to be his secretary. At the time Johnson had little interest in medicine or a college degree. Four months later, he promoted her to research assistant. Although she was classically untrained, Johnson's ability to recruit and gain the trust of a variety of male and female volunteers truly made the *Human Sexual Response* possible. As one female participant explained, "She made me feel that I was not only getting paid but helping my gender as well."

- Seated on a leather lounge chair, a woman, naked except for a pillowcase over her head, rubbed the outside of her vulva with a long, plexiglas penis. Attached to a small camera, this "motor powered phallus," nicknamed Ulysses, could produce high-quality color-motion photographs. Sensors fixed to various parts of the woman's body recorded her heart rate, the electrical impulses of her brain. Nearby sat Masters and Johnson along with their staff, all clad in white cotton coats. When the woman slipped the dildo inside her vagina and climaxed, she allowed researchers a sustained look at her flushed, contracting pussy. Over the next few years this basic experiment would be repeated with hundreds of women. Their findings, published as the *Human Sexual Response* (1966), proved explosive: the female orgasm in full physiological detail.

- A classic romance: less than a year into their professional partnership, Masters made Johnson a proposition: by sleeping together, he reasoned, they could extend their experiments into actual experience, rather than relying on photographic documentation. According to their biographer, Masters saw the arrangement as consensual while she interpreted it, "probably correctly," as a requirement. "Bill did it all—I didn't want him," she later remarked, "I had a job and I wanted it."

- After observing over 600 men and women, Masters and Johnson devised their four-phase description of orgasm: (1) excitement, (2) plateau, (3) orgasm, and (4) resolution. They found that men responded in terms of basic physiological changes along the same lines as women; in both sexes, there was an increase in heart rate, blood pressure, muscle tension, and in the majority, a "sex flush." They also discovered the source of vaginal lubrication, which is plasma seeping through the vaginal walls, as well as uncovering the phenomenon of "vaginal tenting," during which the inner two-thirds of the vagina increases in both length and width, creating a tenting or ballooning effect.

- Masters and Johnson stressed the clit's singular qualities: "The clitoris is a unique organ in the total of human anatomy," they wrote. "No such organ exists within the anatomic structure of the human male."

- *The Human Sexual Response* was alarming precisely because it was so specific, full of irrefutable details. Gershon Legman, for instance, found the very idea of a photographic dildo offensive. In *Rationale of a Dirty Joke*, he wrote: "Paraded as science, intra-vaginal photography of erotic acts is actually a worthless sort of voyeuristic activity." Although much of the team's revelatory findings, such as the primacy of the clitoral orgasm, had been established by Kinsey, and women everywhere, Masters and Johnson were seen as proving their speculations via facts—the perceived infallibility of technology.

- I'm not sure what mysteries Legman thought lurked in the so-called ancient hiding place, but he needn't have worried about their exposure. No photographic dildo could reveal, must less quell, the real terror, also thrill, of sex: you never know what the other person in the room is thinking, or will do. You just don't.

- I, myself, read every dirty book I could find, listened to countless strangers tell me about their love lives, as if I believed that through tireless research, endless plotting, I could be immune, somehow superior to, the sexual struggles that plagued so many others. That is, I wanted be "smart" about sex so when the time came for me to venture into the wild, I could waltz away from whatever encounter, no matter how horrific, with all the phlegmatic cool of James Bond, insouciance of a pin-up, forever smiling into the distance.

- What I know: to be "smart" demands a degree of fallibility. One never possesses full control. There is not always a way *not* to get hurt. Knowledge is invaluable insofar as it can help lessen, if not always prevent, the brunt of the wild instant.

- Perhaps what Legman feared was that publishing large, glossy spreads of the inside of the vagina would expose something about sex, and that sex, once laid bare, would not hold as must interest for us *as sex*.

- But if all fucking has to offer us is mystery, a sense of awe, then we are in a very sorry state.

- Despite all the medical reports, diagrams of diseased labias, hours spent watching a flushed red cunt pulsate on a computer screen, I never lost my sense of wonder. I am never bored by a body.

# BETTER SEX

- With Masters and Johnson—who limited their test subjects to women who orgasmed easily during coitus— and the "sexual revolution" of the sixties that emphasized "free love," there came the reign of the orgasm, which, in turn, created an almost oppressive focus on coming.

- "Why be satisfied with one or two orgasms?" asked Dr. Irene Kassorla in her 1982 bestselling book *Nice Girls Do*. Throughout the 1970's Kassorla had counseled married couples on the healing powers of tender touch and multiorgasmic sex. Kassorla called her therapy "The Pleasure Process," and the methods she employed were similar to techniques pioneered by Masters and Johnson in the 1960's: couples were instructed to spend hours hugging and "fingertipping" (rubbing each other's backs) before sex, often openly discussing their fantasies or repressions, slowly progressing to more intimate touch with penetrative, orgasmic sex as the ultimate goal. "Among the patients who have learned and practiced my techniques," wrote Kassorla, "having as many as a hundred orgasms in a two hour period is not uncommon."

- *Why be satisfied?* The crux of sex liberalism: "better sex" is always possible.

- Note the implicit sense of failure, of exhaustion, before one's even begun.

- Note how in Kasslora's sexual universe bad sex has little to do with good sex because all sex is inherently good. Natural. If Kasslora's philosophy sounds especially utopian, it is not because she envisions a world in which everyone orgasms all time, but rather, she acts as if it were possible to "just fuck."

- Of one thing I am convinced: there is no natural way to exist as a body in the world.

# OUR BODIES, OURSELVES

- When the Women's Health Movement began to flourish in the late sixties and early seventies, the establishment attacked. In 1972 police stormed the Feminist Women's Health clinic in Los Angeles, arresting Carol Downer and Colleen Wilson for practicing medicine without a license. Their transgression: retrieving lost and/or stuck tampons and diaphragms and performing the DIY yeast infection cure of inserting yogurt into the vagina.

- One of the first widely distributed feminist health guides in the United States, *Our Bodies, Ourselves*, covered a range of topics including the clitoris, periods, pregnancy, lesbianism, for-profit healthcare, and getting off. Although written in a consciousness-raising mode, *Our Bodies Ourselves* eschewed outright assertions about the right and wrong ways to be a woman or the "best" method of orgasm. In the chapter on *Love and Relationships*, the authors wrote, "We have no opinion about monogamous or non-monogamous relationships [...] we want to explore the possibilities of getting love and support from several people." Flip over a few pages to find a ten step guide to arm exercise followed by self-defense diagrams instructing women how to use the "knife edge of [the] foot" as a weapon.

- In the mid-seventies multiple parts of the clitoris were also beginning to be labeled in mainstream medical texts due to the success of Masters and Johnson and the feminist movement. As scholars Lisa Jean Moore and Adele E. Clarke have noted, "The impact of the Women's Health Movement cannot be underestimated. They were, in short, fundamentally contesting the ways in which biomedicine had been naturalized."

- Another decisive contestation: *The Hite Report on Female Sexuality*. Published in 1976, *The Hite Report* added to the work of Kinsey and Masters in a crucial way: Shere Hite sought to uncover how individuals regard sexual experience and the meaning it holds for them. "It's not specifically just *orgasms* we are talking about here," Hite wrote, "[but] a complete redefinition, or un-definition, of what sex is."

- Collected from long essay-style questionnaires, *The Hite Report* uses the personal stories of women themselves as the main text. Its very success lies in the glut of personal accounts. To know that women are sexually frustrated is one thing, but to read page after page of "long foreplay makes me uncomfortable because I worry that I'm putting my man through too much work" is quite another. In response to the question, "*How have most men had sex with you?*": "the usual pattern—kiss—feel—eat—fuck."

- All but 5% of heterosexual couples, Hite discovered, followed the "reproductive" model of sex: foreplay (touching, kissing, oral sex), followed by penetration, and intercourse (thrusting) followed by orgasm (especially male orgasm), usually defined as the end of sex.

- Hite also found that 70% of women did not orgasm from intercourse alone. For the majority of women, clitoral stimulation is used for arousal purposes but not orgasm. Through the reproductive model of sex, male orgasm is given a standardized time and place that is prearranged and preagreed upon, during which both people know what to expect. This places women in the position of having to ask for something "special."

- While the 1960's may well have been, as Bill Masters quipped, "the decade of orgasmic preoccupation," this did not necessarily carry over into women's actual experiences. Hite's research showed that an awareness of the mechanics, ease, and potency of female orgasm did not appear to have much effect on the way the majority of women fucked.

- "My lover was bad in bed," however, can sometimes be understood as "I did not tell them what I wanted." Many, however, do tell.

- Consider newlywed Nora Joyce straddling the inexperienced James in bed "like a horse," tenderly urging him, "fuck up, love! fuck up!"

- Or novelist Kathy Acker exhorting her lover: spank my ass, spank anywhere, "just do not touch the clit." In an interview with Andrea Juno, Acker explained, "So the average man who wants to be a non-macho pig wants to go down on you, right?...I try to suggest, 'Why don't you spank me a little?' and they go, 'I couldn't do a thing like that!' And I go, 'Oh yes you could!'"

- When Ella, the main character in Doris Lessing's *The Golden Notebook*, tells her lover that she prefers vaginal orgasm, what she calls "a real orgasm," he scoffs, "Do you know that there are eminent physiologists who say women have no physical basis for vaginal orgasm?" Ella flips her hair: "Then they don't know much, do they?"

- If the sexual revolution of the 1960's conceived of bliss as the best possible orgasm, performance artist Annie Sprinkle's pornographic oeuvre highlighted the inherently exploratory nature of sex, an act with no set methods, expected outcomes, beyond the thrill of you pressed against me.

- *Deep Inside Annie Sprinkle* (1982), Sprinkle's directorial debut, not only championed the clitoris; it also eroticized female ejaculation. While masturbating, during a long, ecstatic multiple orgasm, Sprinkle laughs and moans while her lover graciously laps up her streaming nectar.

- One needn't be young, thin, white or able-bodied to cruise through Sprinkle's erotic universe. Although defenders of mainstream pornography have long praised the medium's diversity—citing the jejune observation that one can find pornography tailored to nearly every desire—othered bodies are rarely treated as anything more than novelties. In Sprinkle's work, however, *all* bodies become subjects, people-touching-people, their bodies honored, if not worshiped.

- I was not born knowing that my body was worth honoring. I had to stumble upon in slowly, stupidly. In a book.

- "Maybe you can give me a sign letting me know what is happening to me," writes Celie, the fourteen year old narrator of Alice Walker's *The Color Purple*, in a letter addressed to God. Although she is unsure if she believes in a god, she doesn't dare tell anyone else about the troubles she's seen. Mentally and sexually abused by her father, Celie is married off to the equally cruel Mr. \_\_\_\_\_. When Shug, Mr. \_\_\_\_\_'s long-time lover, falls ill, she moves in with the couple. As Celie nurses Shug, they begin to "hug, sometimes talk." When Celie describes her years of compulsory sex with Mr. \_\_\_\_\_, Shug laughs, "Why you still a virgin." That is, un-fucked, virtually *untouched* for she has yet to experience a single gasp of personal pleasure.

- "Listen, right down there, in your pussy, is a little button that gits real hot [...] then it melts," Shug says to Celie. Within weeks, they become lovers. The more pleasure she shares with Shug, the more defiant Celie becomes, eventually confronting Mr. ___: "Until you do right by me, everything you touch will crumble."

- As if all she needed was a person, anyone at all, to show her she deserved pleasure, that her body was even capable of recognizing pleasure. One person. Maybe you.

# FEMALE GENITAL OPERATIONS

- The origins of clitoridectomy date back to ancient Egypt, pre-Islamic Arabia, ancient Rome, and Tsarist Russia. According to historian Mary Knight, ancient practitioners possessed a clear understanding of clitoral anatomy and were able to distinguish between the clitoral organ and surrounding tissue.

- In antiquity clitoridectomies were performed for a variety of reasons, most commonly as a remedy for the "overly large clitoris" as described by Sonorus, Galen, and Aetius. The procedure was in-line with the Greco-Roman preoccupation with bodily perfection. Surgery, whether performed before or after death, was one way of attaining the ideal form.

- There are many terms used to refer to modern female genital operations (FGO): clitoridectomy, female genital cutting, female genital mutilation, circumcision, etc. However, the wide diversity of procedures performed in countries as diverse as Sudan, Somalia, Ethiopia, Egypt, Kenya, Nigeria, Mali, Iraq, Yemen, and Aboriginal Australia requires specification. According to UNICEF, 125 million women worldwide have undergone genital operations of some type:

- Circumcision (also known as *sunna* circumcision): The physical operation consists of the removal of the top of the clitoris and is analogues to male circumcision in the West

- Excision (or reduction): removal of the prepuce and glans of clitoris with adjacent parts of the labia minora—or the whole clitoris or labia majora but without the closure of the vulva.

- Circumbustion: removal of entire clitoris by means of charring.

- Infibulation (also known as *pharaonic circumcision*): the most severe method which involves excision of the clitoris itself and potentially portions of the labia minora and majora and the sewing together of the remaining tissues. Women who undergo infibulation typically must be cut open to have sex or give birth.

- Unclassified: includes pricking, piercing or incising of the clitoris and/or labia. For instance, Ancient Romans pierced the genitalia of their female slaves with pins or fibula. Stretching of the clitoris, and surrounding tissue, introduction of corrosive substances or herbs into the vagina to cause bleeding or for the purposes of tightening or narrowing it.

- Before the 1980's genital procedures were routinely referred to as "female genital cutting" (FGC). In 1979, however, Australian feminist Fran P. Hosken coined the phrase "female genital mutilation" (FGM) in *The Hosken Report on Sexual Mutilation*, which focused almost exclusively on infibulation.

- Language is power: within two decades most Western countries had not only adopted Hosken's terminology but also passed laws forbidding its practice; several African nations followed suit. The World Health Organization (WHO) continues to employ the "female genital mutilation" label, defining it as "all procedures that involve partial or total removal of the external female genitalia, or other injury to the female genital organs for non-medical reasons."

- The term "mutilation" itself harkens early 20$^{th}$ century missionary efforts in Kenya where Protestant missionaries began crusading against the practice in 1906. Twenty-three years later, the Kenya Missionary Council began referring to the practice exclusively as "sexual mutilation."

- Despite lingering tension between Western and African feminists over the use of Hosken's phrase, many private health institutions (such as the WHO) continue to employ "mutilation." While genital modification of any kind is an alarming practice, the long-term health effects of traditional female genital operations have been exaggerated in Western media, especially the connection between FGO and obstetric complications. A 2006 WHO study suggested that the risk of complications during pregnancy for women who had undergone milder forms of FGC (excision or circumcision) was less than maternal smoking.

- As a position statement issued by Women's Caucus of the African Studies Association stressed, "The health consequences of clitoridectomy must be located within the larger context in which women's health may also be severely affected by malnutrition, lack of clean water, and inadequate healthcare."

- "Is it, after all, unreasonable," asks Henry Louis Gates in his essay *A Liberalism of Heart and Spine* (1994), "to be suspicious of Westerners who are exercised over female circumcision [in Africa], but whose eyes glaze over when the same women are merely facing starvation?"

- If American women are especially drawn to narratives of "genital mutilation," their interest might very well lie in the fact that sexual violence imbues their daily lives.

- Look closer: female genital operations are declining everywhere except wealthy, Western countries where the desire for a "designer vagina" is spreading.

- Labiaplasty—one of the most popular forms of Female Cosmetic Genital Surgery (FCGS) in the West—involves trimming the inner labia, typically to make them small enough to be concealed by the outer labia.

- In interviews women seeking Labiaplasty most commonly cited a desire for a more aesthetic vulva—one that was "compact," "flat," "tucked in." No one part out of place.

- Other common genital operations include vaginal tightening, vaginal rejuvenation (intended to give the vagina a more "youthful" appearance), hymen reconstruction, liposcution of mons venis, clitoral "lifts," clitoral hood reduction, clitoral repositioning, a G-spot Injections (which enhances G-spot stimulation for up to four months).

- In the United States the number of patients seeking Clitoropexy, or clitoral hood reduction, is increasing. Dr. Altar, a self-professed expert in Clitoropexy, has offices in Beverly Hills and on Park Avenue. He also claims to have developed his own novel technique: Extended Central Wedge Resection, in which a central wedge of V is removed from "the most protrubent portion of each labium minus."

- On his website, Dr. Altar reports that between January 1, 2005 and December 31, 2006, he performed Clitoropexy on a total of 407 patients between the ages of 13 to 65 with an average age of 32.4 years with a self-reported 98% success rate.

- How does one determine the success of Clitoropexy? Sheer smallness of the hood? Overall "neat" appearance? The way it feels rolling between two fingertips?

- While it is commonplace for patients to show pornographic photos to their surgeons to limn their ideal vuvla or clitoris, FGCS is rarely described as a purely aesthetic procedure in medical literature, advertisements, or patient accounts.

Rather, all media about FGCS stressed the potential for better, more satisfying sex.

- Enter Princess Marie leveled out in bed after her third surgery, lifting up the thin cotton sheet to peek at her newly doctored cunt.

- When I looked through the hundreds of before and after photos on surgeon websites, I was not struck by the uniformity of the cunts themselves so much as the way the ideal pussies seemed to fulfill the destiny of sex liberalism itself wherein great sex is defined by easy and frequent orgasms (at whatever cost) and good-in-bed becomes the mark of the authentic, truly liberated woman.

- While both Labiaplasty and Clitoropexy involve extensive modification of labial and clitoral tissue, FCGS is not included in the legal descriptions of "Female Genital Mutilation" adopted by most Western nations. The WHO, for instance, bans even the ritual "pricking" of the female genitals while the current law in the UK explicitly forbids "the partial or total removal of external female genital organs." In practice, however, these laws tend only to apply to women from certain cultural backgrounds, countries, and skin colors.

- Also curiously excluded from legal definitions of FGM in the West is the "management of intersex infants."

- Here, size matters: Clitoral Recession, which involves reducing or covering an enlarged clitoris, is performed in the US and elsewhere on infants born with what surgeons (or overriding cultural norms) deem "ambiguous" genitals.

- Clitoral Recession, developed in 1961 by John Lattimer, remains the most common technique for clitoral reduction on intersex infants. After a chromosome test is performed, if the baby is born XX, the penis is reduced in size, labia are shaped, and a vagina is formed. If the baby tests XY, a decision is made whether to increase the size of the penis through hormone treatment or surgery—or create a clitoris and vagina. A "normal" clitoris at birth is considered by most surgeons to be 1 centimeter and the penis, between 2.5 and 4. If a baby's genitals are between 1 and 2.5 centimeters, they are considered to be ambiguous. Always-already othered.

- Summarizing the beliefs of genital surgeons working with intersex infants, researcher Suzanne Kessler argues that "the most important thing is that the clitoris be small." In her article *Creating Good-Looking Genitals in the Service of Gender*, Kessler highlights the "emotional" language typically used by genital surgeons in medical literature to describe large clitorises: "imperfect," "defective," "malformation," "anatomic derangements," "deformed," "obtrusive," "grossly enlarged," "offending shaft," and "troublesome."

- *Obtrusive...troublesome.* As if the clitoris itself were demanding. As if its main offense is insisting on being seen.

# DIRTY WORDS

- Princess Marie Bonaparte once remarked that the peoples of the world could be thought of as friends or enemies of the clitoris.

- Publisher and right-wing agitator Noel Pemberton-Billing was no friend of the clit. In what British newspapers called "the trial of century," he defended himself against libel charges filed by Maud Allan, the premier erotic dancer of her era. On February 16, 1918, Pemberton-Billing's conservative newspaper, *The Vigilante*, published an inflammatory article entitled, "The Cult of the Clitoris," in which the author accused many public figures, including government officials, of debaucherous sexual behavior, among other things. So ludicrous were the allegations that almost nobody bothered to respond, except Maud Allan.

- The meaning of the article's title "The Cult of the Clitoris" was never made explicit; however, its obscurity was not accidental. On the witness stand the first day of the trial, Captain Spencer, the author of the piece, claimed that he specifically sought a title "that would only be understood by those whom it should be understood by." When Pemberton-Billing asked one witness, an experienced physician, if another word beside "clitoris" could have conveyed the same message in the title, he replied, "No," except, perhaps, "lesbianism." Allan was being accused of lesbianism on the sole premise that she knew the meaning of the word "clitoris."

- In 1975 the clit entered the courts again, during the obscenity trial for *Deep Throat*. Touted as the first porn to feature a plot, *Deep Throat* (1972) concerned a young woman, Linda Lovelace, whose clitoris was located in the back of her throat. The presiding judge, admittedly, had never heard of the clitoris, and although only the lead actor was convicted, prosecutor William Purcell made it very clear that the "obscene" nature of *Deep Throat*, its real "threat" to society, was the clitoral orgasm. Purcell faced the courtroom: "A woman seeing this film may think it is perfectly healthy [to] have a clitoral orgasm. That that is all a woman needs. She is wrong [...] and this film will strengthen her in her ignorance."

- Fast forward to 1994—post-Freud, "post-feminist." When performance artist Holly Hughes' show *CLIT NOTES* debuted, the *New York Times* refused to print the title; instead they referred to the show's name as using a slang term for the word 'clitoris.' Before going on the air on NPR, the radio execs told her that she could use the word clitoris if, and only if, she was referring explicitly to her own clitoris. Hughes wrote, "Under no circumstance, I was warned, could I call someone else a clitoris." As if it were a dirty word.

- A friend asked Hughes why she named the piece *CLIT NOTES*, arguing that "it needs to involve more clit or more notes." The friend claimed that the only reason Hughes used the title was to force people to say the word "clit." "Which was of course, true," wrote Hughes. "I think that making more people wrap their mouths around the word, if not the thing itself, is precisely the kind of political goal one can hope to realize through theater."

- The clitoral effacement extends to Anne Frank's journals. When *The Diary of a Young Girl* was first published in June

1947 roughly thirty percent of its material had been deleted by her father, Otto Frank, at the suggestion of the publisher. The expurgated material included passages in which Anne remarks negatively on her housemates and family as well as a lengthy entry from March 24, 1944 in which she describes her vuvla, clitoris, and vagina from the perspective of her own fifteen year old gaze:

> "Until I was eleven or twelve, I didn't realize there was a second set of labia on the inside, since you couldn't see them. What's even funnier is that I thought urine came out of the clitoris...When you're standing up, all you see from the front is hair. Between your legs there are two soft, cushiony things, also covered with hair, which press together when you're standing, so you can't see what's inside. They separate when you sit down and they're very red and quite fleshy on the inside. In the upper part, between the outer labia, there's a fold of skin that, on second thought, looks like a kind of blister. That's the clitoris."

+ The unabridged edition of Anne Frank's journals was released in 1995, the fiftieth anniversary of her death, with a new translation by Susan Masssotty that included the previously deleted passages. In November 2009, the unabridged version was pulled from the library shelves and classroom bookcases at Culpeper Middle School in Culpeper, Virginia after a parent complained the diary contained explicit sexual content inappropriate for an eighth grade readership.

+ In an email to the *Star-Exponent*, a local Virginia newspaper, school superintendent Bobbi Johnson wrote,"The essence of the story, the struggle of a young girl faced with horrible atrocities, is not lost by editing the few pages that speak to adolescent discovery of intimate feelings."

# RESEARCH

- As a child, the general narrative regarding sex was straightforward: once you reach a certain age, and begin to desire someone, you will feel that sexual itch. As a kid, physical pleasure is beyond you, a far-off paradise, a prize of adulthood. This is presented as a fact rooted in biology: the young body *cannot* experience sexual pleasure. But, of course, human bodies can orgasm at any age, even while *in utero*.

- If I had grown up in the city, it might have been different. But living on a farm, with no neighbors or high-speed internet, my access to pornography was limited. I saw the usual dirty mags, glossy spreads of beaver heaven; as a girl, these still images left me cold as did the sex manuals my friends lifted from their parents and pored over at parties. The pencil-drawn figures seemed as remote and unsexed as the women in the magazines, and they bored me for the same reason as the Saturday-morning cartoons: the characters' bodies were immune to the weather, landscape, time itself. They felt neither pleasure nor pain. What did that have to do with me?

- When I discovered streaming pornography alone in my first apartment, I was already a seasoned masturbator. My curiosity had a specific purpose: I wanted to educate myself, to find out what sort of things other people might want to do with my body, if I let them.

- A common tale: I spent weeks tethered to my laptop. Before long I had cruised beyond the mainstream sites to the realm of "user-uploaded" clips. Although these websites' emphasis on showcasing only "real bodies" peeved me (what were the bodies of porn stars, then?), I also gloried in this newfound domain of overweight, middle-aged couples plowing away in the usual positions, moaning to high heaven, spreading it wide for all to see.

- Most good pornography, like literature, is a rebuttal to "no one wants to see that!": "Oh yes I do!"

- In film pornography I hear and see the impact of every action on the flesh—the smack of balls, squish of a soused pussy, groan of bones as the bodies shift into ever more ludicrous positions. When a woman is asked to perform something painful like, say, fit three dicks inside her vagina at once, she may moan with glee, but her body will tell us otherwise: her pussy (and the skin around it) will swell. If it's a particularly rough fuck, she'll need stitches. In these clips, the body is presented—often despite the producers' best efforts—as *livid*, full of infinite feelings.

- Although thousands of American men get off degrading women on and off film, the topic is not especially intriguing to me intellectually; however, since I possess a clit and cunt, the thought occupies a great deal of my time. In that sense, the question of pornography is not an issue of censorship vs. artistic freedom or the value of erotic art. The question is: why do some men revel in the degradation of women?

- After months of watching, I suspected I had erred: it was not an education I needed but experience.

- I will tell you what I miss: the pleasure of merely eavesdropping. Sitting very still, looking very close. No pressure to think, move, be "of use."

- The comfort of research is legs splayed on the couch, body blasted off in a tender daydream. I know where I am going, where I will end. Whereas to "essay," to write at all, is to set off into the velvety woods without map, without even knowing if it will be worth the trek.

- I started with a question: what does the body want? And ended with: it wants.

- My facts took me no further. It was not my question.

- Which is to say—look again.

- If someone had asked me, when I began researching the clitoris, if I was a writer, I would have said, "No, I'm more of a reader." No matter that I had filled the margins of every book I owned, not with notes, but responses.

- What does it mean, anyway, to be *just* a reader? *Merely* a scholar? Consider my immediate dismissal of the hierarchy between vaginal and clitoral orgasms or good and bad pleasure while clinging, until the very last stages of my research, to the misguided assumption that reading required one kind of intelligence while writing demanded an altogether different variety, one which was, by definition, beyond me.

- A journal entry written when I was seventeen, around the time I discovered Anaïs Nin's diaries: "Nothing can happen to me that someone else has not already described better than I." When I scribbled those lines, I felt a shot of pride, that of a discoverer who has, almost by accident, stumbled upon a new way to make even the most tedious of sunstroked afternoons more sufferable. Only now do I recognize this period as one of my saddest.

- The lesson of the clitoris differs person to person. Some learn that the asshole is as ripe a source of bliss as the clit. Others, the importance of intuition, of listening to their body, to what they alone can verify as a fact, if not a truth. For me, the lesson of the clitoris remains: how can I understand what happens to me if I do not say it?

# SELECTED BIBLIOGRAPHY

## BOOKS

*A New View of a Woman's Body*, Federation of Feminist Women's Health Center

*Anais: The Erotic Life of Anais Nin*, Noël Riley Fitch

*Angry Women*, Andrea Juno

*Bastard Out of Carolina*, Dorothy Allison

*Breaking the Chain: Women, Theory, and French Realist Fiction*, Naomi Schor

*The Clitoral Truth*, Rebecca Chalker

*The Clitoris*, Thomas Lowry and Thea Lowry

*The Complete Clitoris*, Thomas Lowry

*Eve's Secrets: A New Theory of Female Sexuality*, Josephine Sevely. 1987.

*Funny Peculiar: Gershon Legman and the Psychopathology of Humor*, Mikita Brottman

*The G Spot and Other Recent Discoveries about Human Sexuality*, Alice Kahn Ladas, Beverly Whipple and John D. Perry

*Hannah Wilke: Gestures*, Tracy Fitzpatrick with Saundra Goldman, Tom Kochheiser, Griselda Pollock

*The Hite Report: a Nationwide Study of Female Sexuality*, Shere Hite

*The Hosken Report*, Fran Hosken

*Human Sexual Response*, William Masters and Virginia Johnson

*The Kinsey Report: Sexual Behavior in the Human Female*, Alfred Kinsey

*La Bâtarde*, Violette Leduc

*Love Between Women: Early Christian Responses to Female Homoeroticism*, Bernadette J. Brooten

*Making Sex: Body and Gender from the Greeks to Freud*, Thomas Laqueur

*Marie Bonaparte: A Life*, Celia Bertin

*Masters of Sex: The Life and Times of William Masters and Virginia Johnson, the Couple Who Taught America How to Love*, Thomas Maier

*The Nature and Evolution of Female Sexuality*, Mary Jane Sherfey

*Nice Girls Do*, Irene Kassorla

*Nora: The Real Life of Molly Bloom*, Brenda Maddox

*Oragentalism*, Gershon Legman

*Oscar Wilde's Last Stand*, Philip Hoare

*Our Bodies, Ourselves*, Boston Women's Health Clinic (1973)

*The Renaissance of Lesbianism in Early Modern England*, Valerie Traub

*Reading in Detail: Aesthetics and the Feminine*, Naomi Schor

*The Sexual Life of Catherine M*, Catherine Millet

*Sex the Measure of All Things: A Life of Alfred C Kinsey*, Jonathan Gathorne-Hardy

*Sexual Variance in Society and History* Vern L Bullough

*Simone de Beauvoir: A Biography*, Deirdre Bair

*Solitary Sex: A Cultural History of Masturbation*, Thomas W. Laqueur

*The Color Purple*, Alice Walker

*The Golden Notebook*, Doris Lessing

*The Technology of Orgasm: "Hysteria," the Vibrator, and Women's Sexual Satisfaction*, Rachel P. Maines

*Three Essays on the Theory of Sexuality*, Sigmund Freud

## ARTICLES

"Anatomy of the Clitoris," Helen E. O'Connell, K.V. Sanjeenvan, J.M. Huston. *Journal of Urology*

"Clitoral Conventions and Transgressions: Graphic Representations in Anatomy Texts, c1900-199," Lisa Jean Moore and Adele E. Clarke

"Creating Good-Looking Genitals in the Service of Gender," Suzanne Kessler

"Critical Clitoridectomy: Female Sexual Imagery and Feminist Psychoanalytic Theory," Paula Bennett

"Curing Cut or Ritual Mutilation?: Some Remarks on the Practice of Female and Male Circumcision in Graeco-Roman Egypt," Mary Knight

"Female Genital Cosmetic Surgery: A Critical Review of Current Knowledge and Contemporary Debates," Virgina Braun

"Female Genital Mutilation: Whose Problem, Whose Solution?," Ronán M Conroy

"Female Homoeroticism and the Denial of Roman Reality in Latin Literature," Judith P. Hallett (from *Roman Sexualities*)

"In Search of (Better) Sexual Pleasure: Female Genital 'Cosmetic' Surgery," Virgina Braun

"Labia Reduction for Non-therapeutic Reasons vs. Female Genital Mutilation: Contradictions in Law and Practice in Britain," Marge Berer

"Nonreproductive Sexual Behavior: Ethological and Cultural Considerations," Ina Jane Wundram

*"Searching for "Voices": Feminism, Anthropology, and the Global Debate over Female Genital Operations,"* Christine J. Walley

"Sexing the Hyena: Intraspecies Readings of the Female Phallus," Anna Wilson

"Uncoding Mama: The Female Body as Text," Robert Scholes (from *Semiotics and Interpretation*)

"Virgin Territory: The Male Discovery of the Clitoris," Nancy Scheper-Hughes

## QUOTES

"The question is: why do some men revel in the degradation of women?," Jeanette Winterson, *The Mystique of Henry Miller*

"the body can no longer stand to be a body at all," Clarice Lispector, *Agua Viva*

# ACKNOWLEDGEMENTS

This book would not exist without the guidance and support of Carey Hall, Janet Sarbanes, Amanda Montei, Allie Rowbottom, and the entire writing community at CalArts.

Deep gratitude to Jessalyn Wakefield, Jessica Hallock, and Claire Cramer for your friendship and your livejournals.

Most of all thank you to M for love and magic and never falling asleep before me.

Selections from this book have appeared in *Among Margins: an Anthology of Aesthetics*, *Best Experimental Writing*, *LIT*, *P-QUEUE*, and on the Les Figues Press blog.

## ABOUT THE AUTHOR

Elizabeth Hall lives on a crumbling bluff in San Pedro, California. She is the author of the chapbook *Two Essays* (eohippus labs) and plays bass in the band Pine Family.

# TARPAULIN SKY PRESS
Current Titles (2016)

hallucinatory ... trance-inducing (***Publishers Weekly* "Best Summer Reads"**); warped from one world to another (***The Nation***); somewhere between Artaud and Lars Von Trier (***VICE***); simultaneously metaphysical and visceral ... scary, sexual, and intellectually disarming (***Huffington Post***); only becomes more surreal (***NPR Books***); horrifying and humbling in their imaginative precision (***The Rumpus***); wholly new (***Iowa Review***); breakneck prose harnesses the throbbing pulse of language itself (***Publishers Weekly***); the opposite of boring.... an ominous conflagration devouring the bland terrain of conventional realism (***Bookslut***); creating a zone where elegance and grace can gambol with the just-plain-fucked-up (***HTML Giant***); both devastating and uncomfortably enjoyable (***American Book Review***); consistently inventive (***TriQuarterly***); playful, experimental appeal (***Publishers Weekly***); a peculiar, personal music that is at once apart from and very much surrounded by the world (***Verse***); a world of wounded voices (***Hyperallergic***); dangerous language, a murderous kind.... discomfiting, filthy, hilarious, and ecstatic (***Bookslut***); dark, multivalent, genre-bending ... unrelenting, grotesque beauty (***Publishers Weekly***); futile, sad, and beautiful (***NewPages***); refreshingly eccentric (***The Review of Contemporary Fiction***); a kind of nut job's notebook (***Publishers Weekly***); thought-provoking, inspired and unexpected. Highly recommended (***After Ellen***).

Set in a decaying town in southern West Virginia, this debut novel from Steven Dunn, *Potted Meat*, follows a young boy into adolescence as he struggles with abusive parents, poverty, alcohol addiction, and racial tensions. Using fragments as a narrative mode to highlight the terror of ellipses, *Potted Meat* explores the fear, power, and vulnerability of storytelling, and in doing so, investigates the peculiar tensions of the body: How we seek to escape or remain embodied during repeated trauma. "Steven Dunn's *Potted Meat* is full of wonder and silence and beauty and strangeness and ugliness and sadness and truth and hope. I am so happy it is in the world. This book needs to be read" (**LAIRD HUNT**). "*Potted Meat* is an extraordinary book. Here is an emerging voice that calls us to attention. I have no doubt that Steven Dunn's writing is here, like a visceral intervention across the surface of language, simultaneously cutting to its depths, to change the world. My first attempt at offering words in this context was to write: thank you. And that is how I feel about Steven Dunn's writing; I feel grateful: to be alive during the time in which he writes books" (**SELAH SATERSTROM**).

Dana Green's debut collection of stories, *Sometimes the Air in the Room Goes Missing*, explores how storytelling changes with each iteration, each explosion, each mutation. Told through multiple versions, these are stories of weapons testing, sheep that can herd themselves into watercolors, and a pregnant woman whose water breaks every day for nine months — stories told with an unexpected syntax and a sense of déjà vu: narrative as echo. "I love Dana Green's wild mind and the beautiful flux of these stories. Here the wicked simmers with the sweet, and reading is akin to watching birds. How lucky, and how glad I am, to have this book in my hands" **(NOY HOLLAND)**. "Dana Green's *Sometimes the Air in the Room Goes Missing* is a tour de force of deeply destabilizing investigation into language and self, languages and selves — for the multiplicities abound here. Excitingly reminiscent at times of the work of Diane Williams and Robert Walser and Russel Edson, Green's brilliant writing is also all her own. This book is the start of something special" **(LAIRD HUNT)**. "Language becomes a beautiful problem amid the atomic explosions and nuclear families and strange symmetries and southwestern deserts and frail human bodies blasted by cancer that comprise Dana Green's bracing debut, which reminds us every ordinary moment, every ordinary sentence, is an impending emergency" **(LANCE OLSEN)**.

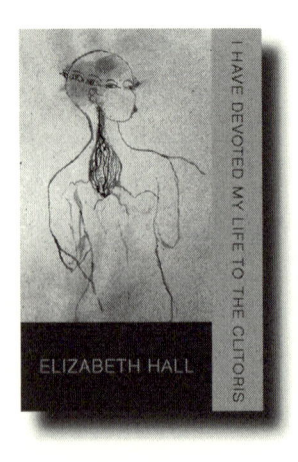

Debut author Elizabeth Hall began writing *I Have Devoted My Life to the Clitoris* after reading Thomas Laqueur's *Making Sex*. She was struck by Laqueur's bold assertion: "More words have been shed, I suspect, about the clitoris, than about any other organ, or at least, any organ its size." If Lacquer's claim was correct, where was this trove of prose devoted to the clit? And more: what did size have to do with it? Hall set out to find all that had been written about the clit past and present. As she soon discovered, the history of the clitoris is no ordinary tale; rather, its history is marked by the act of forgetting. "Marvelously researched and sculpted.... Bulleted points rat-tat-tatting the patriarchy, strobing with pleasure" (**DODIE BELLAMY**). "Freud, terra cotta cunts, hyenas, anatomists, and Acker, mixed with a certain slant of light on a windowsill and a leg thrown open invite us… Bawdy and beautiful" (**WENDY C. ORTIZ**). "Gorgeous little book about a gorgeous little organ… Mines discourses as varied as sexology, plastic surgery, literature and feminism to produce an eye-opening compendium.... The 'tender button' finally gets its due" (**JANET SARBANES**). "God this book is glorious.... You will learn and laugh and wonder why it took you so long to find this book" (**SUZANNE SCANLON**).

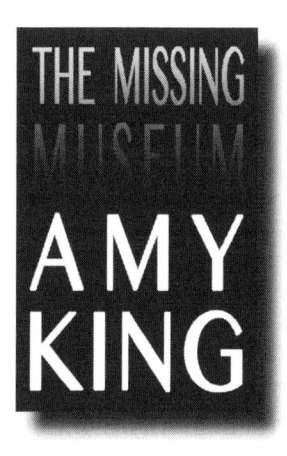

Nothing that is complicated may ever be simplified, but rather catalogued, cherished, exposed. *The Missing Museum*, by acclaimed poet Amy King, spans art, physics & the spiritual, including poems that converse with the sublime and ethereal. They act through ekphrasis, apostrophe & alchemical conjuring. They amass, pile, and occasionally flatten as matter is beaten into text. Here is a kind of directory of the world as it rushes into extinction, in order to preserve and transform it at once. King joins the ranks of Ann Patchett, Eleanor Roosevelt & Rachel Carson as the recipient of the 2015 Women's National Book Association Award. She serves on the executive board of VIDA: Women in Literary Arts and is currently co-editing the anthologies *Big Energy Poets of the Anthropocene: When Ecopoets Think Climate Change*, and *Bettering American Poetry 2015*. Of King's previous collection, *I Want to Make You Safe* (Litmus Press), John Ashbery describes Amy King's poems as bringing "abstractions to brilliant, jagged life, emerging into rather than out of the busyness of living." *Safe* was one of *Boston Globe*'s Best Poetry Books of 2011.

**THE GROTESQUE CHILD**
*a novel by*
**KIM PARKO**

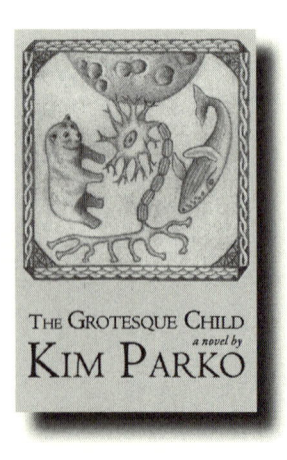

*The Grotesque Child* is a story about being and being and being something else. It is about swallowing and regurgitating, conceiving and birthing. It is about orifices and orbs. It is about the viscous, weepy, goopy, mucousy, bloody state of feminine being and trans-being. It is about pain and various healers and torturers, soothers and inflictors. It is about what sleeps and hides in all the nooks and crannies of perceived existence and existence unperceived. Kim Parko is the author of *Cure All*, published by Caketrain Press. She lives with her husband, daughter, and the seen and unseen, in Santa Fe, New Mexico where she is an associate professor at the Institute of American Indian Arts. Praise for *Cure All*: "Parko's work flickers with pieces of word wizardry while igniting a desire to absorb the strange and distorted.... Giving insight into the human mind and heart is what Parko does best" (**DIAGRAM**)

A Small Press Distribution Bestseller and Staff Pick, chosen by Dennis Cooper for his "Favorite Nonfiction of 2015," and chosen by *Fabulously Feminist Magazine* for its "Nonfiction Books You Need to Read," Aaron Apps's *Intersex* explores gender as it forms in concrete and unavoidable patterns in the material world. What happens when a child is born with ambiguous genitalia? What happens when a body is normalized? *Intersex* provides tangled and shifting answers to both of these questions as it questions our ideas of what is natural and normal about gender and personhood. In this hybrid-genre memoir, intersexed author Aaron Apps adopts and upends historical descriptors of hermaphroditic bodies such as "freak of nature," "hybrid," "imposter," "sexual pervert," and "unfortunate monstrosity" in order to trace his own monstrous sex as it perversely intertwines with gender expectations and medical discourse. "*Intersex* is all feral prominence: a physical archive of the 'strange knot.' Thus: necessarily vulnerable, brave and excessive.... I felt this book in the middle of my own body. Like the best kind of memoir, Apps brings a reader close to an experience of life that is both 'unattainable' and attentive to 'what will emerge from things.' In doing so, he has written a book that bursts from its very frame" (**BHANU KAPIL**).

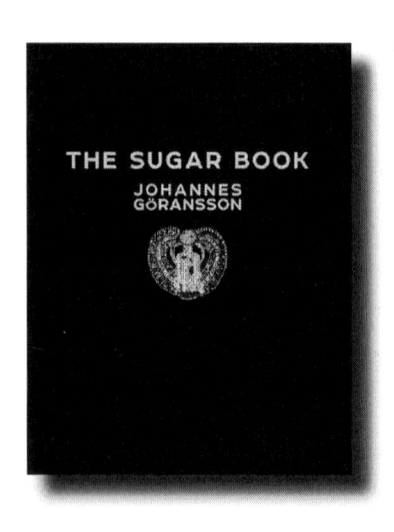

Johannes Goransson's *The Sugar Book* marks the author's third title with TS Press, following his acclaimed *Haute Surveillance* and *entrance to a colonial pageant in which we all begin to intricate*. "Doubling down on his trademark misanthropic imagery amid a pageantry of the unpleasant, Johannes Göransson strolls through a violent Los Angeles in this hybrid of prose and verse…. The motifs are plentiful and varied … pubic hair, Orpheus, law, pigs, disease, Francesca Woodman … and the speaker's hunger for cocaine and copulation….. Fans of Göransson's distorted poetics will find this a productive addition to his body of work" (**PUBLISHERS WEEKLY**); "Sends its message like a mail train. Visceral Surrealism. His end game is an exit wound" (**FANZINE**); "As savagely anti-idealist as Burroughs or Guyotat or Ballard. Like those writers, he has no interest in assuring the reader that she or he lives, along with the poet, on the right side of history" (**ENTROPY MAGAZINE**); "convulses wildly like an animal that has eaten the poem's interior and exterior all together with silver" (**KIM HYESOON**); "'I make a language out of the bleed-through.' Göransson sure as fuck does. These poems made me cry. So sad and anxious and genius and glarey bright" (**REBECCA LOUDON**).

**BURIAL**
*Claire Donato*

The debut novella from Claire Donato that rocked the small press world. "Poetic, trance-inducing language turns a reckoning with the confusion of mortality into readerly joy at the sensuality of living." (*PUBLISHERS WEEKLY* "BEST SUMMER READS"). "A dark, multivalent, genre-bending book.... Unrelenting, grotesque beauty an exhaustive recursive obsession about the unburiability of the dead, and the incomprehensibility of death" (*PUBLISHERS WEEKLY* STARRED REVIEW). "Dense, potent language captures that sense of the unreal that, for a time, pulls people in mourning to feel closer to the dead than the living.... [S]tartlingly original and effective" (*MINNEAPOLIS STAR-TRIBUNE*). "A grief-dream, an attempt to un-sew pain from experience and to reveal it in language" (*HTML GIANT*). "A full and vibrant illustration of the restless turns of a mind undergoing trauma.... Donato makes and unmakes the world with words, and what is left shimmers with pain and delight" (**BRIAN EVENSON**). "A gorgeous fugue, an unforgettable progression, a telling I cannot shake" (**HEATHER CHRISTLE**). "Claire Donato's assured and poetic debut augurs a promising career" (**BENJAMIN MOSER**).

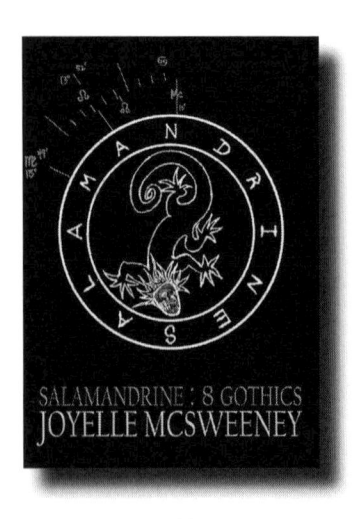

Following her debut novel from Tarpauin Sky Press, the acclaimed SPD bestseller *Nylund, The Sarcographer*, comes Joyelle McSweeney's first collection of short stories, *Salamandrine: 8 Gothics*. "Vertiginous.... Denying the reader any orienting poles for the projected reality.... McSweeney's breakneck prose harnesses the throbbing pulse of language itself" (***PUBLISHERS WEEKLY***). "Biological, morbid, fanatic, surreal, McSweeney's impulses are to go to the rhetoric of the maternity mythos by evoking the spooky, sinuous syntaxes of the gothic and the cleverly constructed political allegory. [A]t its core is the proposition that writing the mother-body is a viscid cage match with language and politics in a declining age.... [T]his collection is the sexy teleological apocrypha of motherhood literature, a siren song for those mothers 'with no soul to photograph'" (***THE BROOKLYN RAIL***). "[L]anguage commits incest with itself.... Sounds repeat, replicate, and mutate in her sentences, monstrous sentences of aural inbreeding and consangeous consonants, strung out and spinning like the dirtiest double-helix, dizzy with disease...." (***QUARTERLY WEST***).

## HOSPITALOGY
## DAVID WOLACH

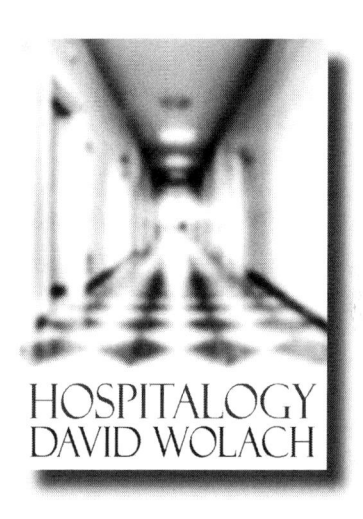

david wolach's fourth book of poetry, *Hospitalogy*, traces living forms of intimate and militant listening within the Hospital Industrial Complex—hospitals, medical clinics and neighboring motels—performing a sociopoetic surgery that is exploratory, not curative. "An extraordinary work.... [A] radical somatics, procedural anatomic work, queer narrativity—where 'the written is explored as catastrophe and its aftermath'" (**ERICA KAUFMAN**). "Dear 'distractionary quickie,' Dear 'groundwater,' Dear 'jesus of the pain.' Welcome to david wolach's beautiful corrosion, *Hospitalogy*" (**FRED MOTEN**). "At a time when hospitality is increasingly deployed to sterilize policies of deportation and incarceration...david wolach performs the common detention of patients, workers, and other undesirables in 'places of liquidation' (**ELENI STECOPOULOS**). "This is a book that documents the soft rebellion of staying alive, articulating the transition from invisibility to indecipherability" (**FRANK SHERLOCK**).

In her second SPD bestseller from Tarpaulin Sky Press, *not merely because of the unknown that was stalking toward them*, Jenny Boully presents a "deliciously creepy" swan song from Wendy Darling to Peter Pan, as Boully reads between the lines of J. M. Barrie's *Peter and Wendy* and emerges with the darker underside, with sinister and subversive places. *not merely because of the unknown* explores, in dreamy and dark prose, how we love, how we pine away, and how we never stop loving and pining away. "This is undoubtedly the contemporary re-treatment that Peter Pan deserves.... Simultaneously metaphysical and visceral, these addresses from Wendy to Peter in lyric prose are scary, sexual, and intellectually disarming" (***Huffington Post***). "[T]o delve into Boully's work is to dive with faith from the plank — to jump, with hope and belief and a wish to see what the author has given us: a fresh, imaginative look at a tale as ageless as Peter himself" (***Bookslut***). "Jenny Boully is a deeply weird writer—in the best way" (**Ander Monson**).

# MORE FROM TARPAULIN SKY PRESS

## FULL-LENGTH BOOKS

Jenny Boully, *[one love affair]**

Ana Božičević, *Stars of the Night Commute*

Traci O Connor, *Recipes for Endangered Species*

Mark Cunningham, *Body Language*

Danielle Dutton, *Attempts at a Life*

Sarah Goldstein, *Fables*

Johannes Göransson, *Entrance to a colonial pageant in which we all begin to intricate*

Noah Eli Gordon & Joshua Marie Wilkinson, *Figures for a Darkroom Voice*

Gordon Massman, *The Essential Numbers 1991 - 2008*

Joyelle McSweeney, *Nylund, The Sarcographer*

Joanna Ruocco, *Man's Companions*

Kim Gek Lin Short, *The Bugging Watch & Other Exhibits*

Shelly Taylor, *Black-Eyed Heifer*

Max Winter, *The Pictures*

Andrew Zornoza, *Where I Stay*

CHAPBOOKS

Sandy Florian, *32 Pedals and 47 Stops*

James Haug, *Scratch*

Claire Hero, *Dollyland*

Paula Koneazny, *Installation*

Paul McCormick, *The Exotic Moods of Les Baxter*

Teresa K. Miller, *Forever No Lo*

Jeanne Morel, *That Crossing Is Not Automatic*

Andrew Michael Roberts, *Give Up*

Brandon Shimoda, *The Inland Sea*

Chad Sweeney, *A Mirror to Shatter the Hammer*

Emily Toder, *Brushes With*

G.C. Waldrep, *One Way No Exit*

&

# Tarpaulin Sky Literary Journal
*in print and online*

tarpaulinsky.com